THE LOWER OUSE VALLEY

Lewes to Newhaven ~

A history of the Brookland

© Margaret Thorburn 2007

THE LOWER OUSE VALLEY
Lewes to Newhaven ~ A history of the Brookland

ISBN   978-0-955242-0-2

Published by Withy Books
43 Cluny Steet
Lewes
East Sussex
BN7 1LN

A CIP catalogue record of this book
can be obtained from the British Library.

Designed & produced by:
The Better Book Company Ltd
Forum House
Stirling Road
Chichester
West Sussex
PO19 7DN

Printed in England

Drainage ditch in The Levels, north of Upper Rise.
Caburn to east.

THE LOWER OUSE VALLEY

Lewes to Newhaven ~

A history of the Brookland

MARGARET THORBURN

WITHY BOOKS

CONTENTS

LIST OF ILLUSTRATIONS

BLACK AND WHITE maps

COLOUR PLATES in centre of book

Colour photographs by the author.

ABBREVIATIONS

ESRO	East Sussex Record Office
WSRO	West Sussex Record Office
SAC	Sussex Archaeological Collections
SRS	Sussex Record Society
SRA	Sussex River Board
SWA	Sussex Water Authority
HMSO	Her Majesty's Stationery Office

ACKNOWLEDGEMENTS

Guidance and conversations have been appreciated with John Bleach, also Christopher Whittick, John Farrant and Colin Brent. Staff at East Sussex Record Office have provided invaluable assistance. I particularly wish to thank Susan Rowland for Figure 5 and Hazel Lintoff for Figure 1. Especially appreciated is the supportive interest from my family and friends.

PREFACE

The smooth skyline shaped by the surrounding downland and the flowing river with the two Rises are the only truly natural features in the Lower Ouse valley. The rest of the landscape formed by fields, hedges, trees, ditches, dykes, quarries, houses, offices, landfill, waste and amenity tips, churches and the castle, pylons and railways and, of course, roads, are all caused by the hand of man. Yet there is a harmony in this landscape as the scale is wide and expansive, with the hint of knowing that, as the view leads south, it will end at the bright sea-waters of the Channel and the stunning white chalk cliffs.

As an incomer to live here in the 1970s, I can still remember the delight of driving along the west side of the valley, parallel to the line of the downs, with the expanse of the brooklands and the extensive arable fields catching the eye. At that time there were large herds of dairy cows munching the lush abundant grass of the brooklands. Sheep on the higher downland were not so visible. It was, and still is, visually lovely – a special landscape. But it was some years later that, thanks to Continuing Education Courses at the University of Sussex, studies gave me the tools to interpret the landscape and to give a depth of understanding to visual appreciation.

The excitement of unfolding documents as stiff and as new as when first written was an unexpected pleasure. Maps and plans are equally a delight – tithe maps, enclosure awards, estate plans, and all those plans of the river drawn for the Commission of Sewers. Manorial court books are rich sources, though not by any means easy to read or interpret. Wills and inventories give insights into people's lives, and sometimes, with luck, can be matched to existing houses. Often the words can be read well enough, but what do they really signify? For instance, those initialled silver rings, so meaningfully designated in wills, proved to be tokens for the exchange of deep friendship between families and friends.

Latterly the gift of a series of Wednesday evening classes at the college in Lewes, inspired by John Bleach, focussing on the Lower Ouse valley, stimulated and matched my interest in this particular landscape area. He came on his bicycle always loaded with books and a tantalising array of material, to whet our curiosity to discover, read and go out, and to observe. This led me to a particular map of

Cliffe with its five sewers, and then to the series of big books holding the records of the Commission of Sewers. Hours were spent in the Record Office at Lewes, painstakingly writing notes that eventually could be sorted to make a history of the brooklands.

The importance of controlling the influx of water from the sea and the sky in this particular environment of the Lower Ouse appears in records from the 10th century onwards. But the thick layers of alluvium of the Lower Ouse have provided core samples, which reveal evidence of denudation from the surrounding earlier landscape, revealing how significant were the effects of human and livestock activities. Also, analysis of colluvium from archaeological sites has produced dateable pottery and bones, which, together with work on snail-type presence and vegetative samples, contributes to interpreting the prehistoric environment, as to how it was used and adapted. Achieving control in the brookland with dykes, ditches and sluices ensured fresh water to nourish lush grass and hay, a key factor in the agrarian balance of meadow, arable and downland pasture. Well nourished livestock meant nourished crops and nourished families. In present time there has been a significant shift from primary products of the brookland to secondary and imported goods of the High Street shops. Successful farms of very recent years are being pressurised into alternative crops and diversification. The value of the brookland pasture has declined, and there have been some changes to other uses such as bird reserves, fishing lakes, horse and pony paddocks and 'set-aside' to overgrown and marshy areas. There is the possibility of certain areas being used to flood permanently.

Pressures on the landscape from urban living are problematic. Gone out of use are the former disfiguring cement works and ugly buildings. But the landfill as Asham scars and distorts the slope of the escarpment. Newhaven expands and there is the vexed question of siting a waste-burning incinerator on former brookland. A rectangle of highways encompasses the Lower Ouse landscape. In the 1970s a new trunk road was made for the A27 to cross The Levels on a chalk causeway. A new bridge spans the Ouse in Lewes, and industrial units cover Malling Brooks. Another new swing bridge crosses the Ouse at Newhaven. One disadvantage of gaining an historical perspective for a landscape is that any change so easily carried out by powerful machinery can be a disturbing event. Hopefully the following pages will give understanding, and also a sense of value, for what has been made for us by past efforts.

The ancient environment

The Lower Ouse valley has in prehistory, not been as it is now, and this account starts with some data on the earlier period of the last glacial period when sea levels were low. As the ice caps melted and retreated, rising sea levels flooded the river valley. R. Castleden in *Classic Landforms of the South Coast* (1996) succinctly describes the probable environment of this period. The first source in order to understand the geology and structure of the Lower Ouse valley is found in the British Geological Survey, The Wealden District (HMSO 1965) and especially 'Pleistocene and Recent Deposits', which includes the formation of river terraces. Articles written and presented to a symposium of British Geographers (1971) at the University of Sussex by D.K.C. Jones and A. Thorley contain data of past environments, analysing sediments in the river valley. By 4000BC hunter/gatherers, pastoralists and farmers had utilised the surrounding downland. Analysis of the work of A. Thorley by P. Drewett, D. Rudling and M. Gardiner in *South East to* AD1000 (1988) 28, demonstrated that lenses of peat deposits in the Vale of Brooks south of Lewes, were being laid down during wet periods between 7000BC-4000BC, within the deposits of marine alluvium. These lenses of peat contained pollens reflecting a well wooded surrounding landscape at this period, containing *alnus* (alder) and also *pinus* (pine). It is suggested that the lighter soils associated with a widespread distribution of loess could have made pine trees possible.

Another study by M.J. Allen (SAC 143 [2005] 35-46) in a coombe at Ashcombe revealed periglacial marl, evidence of tree clearance, agricultural activity and subsequent soil denudation during the Neolithic period c.4000BC. Further work at Southerham and Malling Hill provided samples of deciduous woodland, before 4000BC growing hawthorn, oak, hazel and some pine. By the early Bronze Age, c.1600BC, barrows scattered the downland, also field systems which can be seen at Saxon Down on Malling Down showing evidence of a cleared landscape, (SAC 133 [1995] 19-44).

Loess is recorded again in sediments further north in the Ouse valley at Sharpsbridge. Study of sediments in this location by R. Scaife and P. Burrin (*SAC121 [1983] 1-10*) found a 4cm cover of loess over the region in the post-glacial period. Their study presents indications that grassland and cultivation may have started quite early which 'fits well' with archaeological data for the primary settlement of farming communities in the period around 4000BC. Interestingly this non-tidal river environment, fed by many tributaries and with surrounding woodland is an area with many *feld* names of the later Saxon settlement time, i.e. 'field, open country' (M. Gelling, [2000], 269-279).

More recently M. Waller of the Caburn project (1996-1998) (*SAC* 137, 18) has produced a core in the brookland at the base of The Caburn with pollen evidence showing that *taxus* (yew) grew abundantly on the adjacent slopes. (Yew does not show in the Evans/ Thorley core evidence.) Another recent study in the Bishopstone area (Past and Present No. 98, *SAC* December 2002) by B. Pears confirmed that the valley was once a tidal inlet and subsequently filled with marine alluvium. The infilling of former tidal inlets all along the Sussex Coast, and the relatively quick development of shingle banks across river mouths by west to east longshore drift, is a phenomenon which extends into the historical period. All the core studies agree that anthropogenic deforestation has contributed layers of sedimentation to the alluvial fill in the river valleys since Neolithic times.

During the pre-glacial period (12,000BP), on the north facing slopes of the downland, short indented coombes formed under severe freeze-thaw conditions. Subsequent sludging flowed down the lower slopes and spread over the river terraces as fans of chalky marl known as 'head'. The Solid and Drift editions, no. 318/319, of the Geological Survey show these spreads of 'head' at the scarpfoot on the west side of the Lower Ouse valley, and also to the north at the foot of the north facing scarp at Beddingham – Firle, and Offham – Hamsey, and Malling Down – Stoneham. These spreads of 'head' provided particularly fertile light soils for arable crops, in conjunction with pastoral stock-keeping which are the focus of the following pages describing the brooklands, farming and settlement in the Lower Ouse valley.

Description of the Lower Ouse Valley

South of Lewes there lies an extensive area of 6000 acres (2400 ha) of low ground, below 5 m, known as The Levels. It is an area of deep marine alluvium (12 m – 30 m) infilling the eroded Beddingham to Kingston anticline. Two humps of higher ground, the Upper Rise (21 m) and Lower Rise (26 m) OE *eg* – 'island', are evidence of the underlying Greensand and Gault of the exposed areas of the eroded anticline.

The main river, with heightened banks, flows on the east side of The Levels. Glynde Reach, a misfit river, flowing from the east and Laughton Levels, joins the river Ouse south of Southerham (Glynde – perhaps 'opening in a wood', Reach OE *ric*, brook or ditch). Further south where Asham is situated on the east side and Rodmell on the west side, the river Ouse flows through a narrower valley between the Chalk downland to the sea at Newhaven.

The river in the Lower Ouse valley is now considerably embanked since flood prevention work was constructed from the 18th century onwards. The alluvial brookland is criss-crossed with drainage ditches, sewers and control sluices. During the earlier Saxon period the Lower Ouse would probably have been a braided tidal estuary with salt marshes. The river terraces covered with head from Southover to Rodmell on the west side at above the 5m level, provided 'narrow ribbons of easily worked fertile soils' and provided desirable early settlement sites.

Extending from Southover southwards for 7 miles (12 km) there is a sequence of settlements at ½ mile (1 km) intervals. Southover on a low Chalk promontory was the site of a 6th century Saxon cemetry, and also later to the east, the Cluniac Priory was founded on the site of a Saxon church or minster[1]. To the south west there are the settlements of Kingston, Swanborough, Norton and Sutton at Iford, Northease, Rodmell, Southease, Deans (*Harpingden*), *Orlswick* (now absorbed), Piddinghoe and Meeching (now Newhaven). Seaford on the coast was formerly a port and sea outlet for the Ouse in the medieval period. Bishopstone lies up a former tidal valley in the

---

1 All footnotes appear at the end of the book between pages 42 to 48.

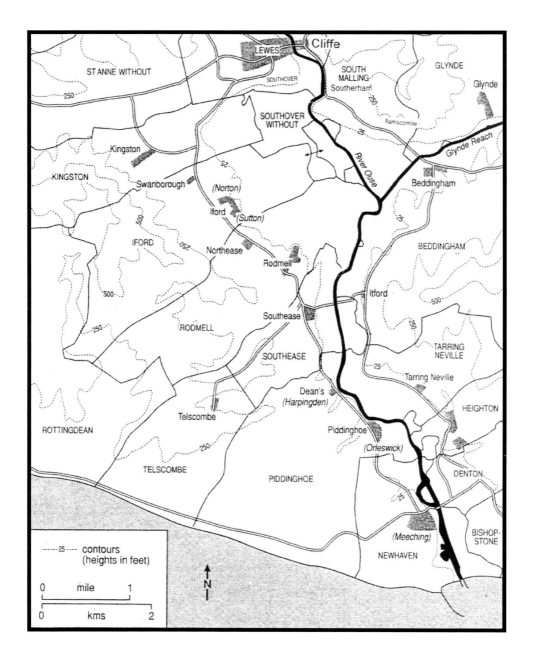

*Fig 1: Settlements in the Lower Ouse valley
and parish boundaries*

downland, and has a church, probably a minster church, with an 8th century *porticus* and evidence of long and short Saxon work in the nave.

A fording point lay between Meeching and the marshland at Denton, probably with a causeway, and gave access to the settlements situated on Lower Chalk shoulders at Denton, South Heighton and Tarring Neville, with extensive marshland below. On the east side of the Lower Ouse there is an absence of river terraces and fewer settlements which at present time are single farmsteads, except for Denton and South Heighton which have become eastward extensions of the commercial development of Newhaven with its port and ferry activities and light industries.

Itford is sited at a narrow fording point on the south margin of The Levels. At Beddingham, Courthouse farm and church, lie on a 5 m (15 ft) promontory above low ground on all sides. Close to the Ouse and Glynde Reach, Ranscombe and Southerham are sited opposite on the edge of the Chalk downland of the Caburn, with extensive brookland below[2].

Prehistoric Period

The Sites and Monuments Data Base at the Archaeology Department of East Sussex County Council in Lewes holds records of all the known finds and locations in East Sussex. In this area under discussion the earliest monument is a causewayed enclosure on Offham Hill, just north of Lewes. To the east over the river a Neolithic long barrow overlooks the environment to the north from Malling Down. Another long barrow, Money Burgh, on a low shoulder (30 m) overlooks the valley from Deans (*OE Harpingden*) to Itford Hill, on which there is a Bronze Age settlement and burial site. Rookery Hill, between Bishopstone and the coast, has been investigated with a detailed report and revealed an extended period of use from the Bronze Age to the early Saxon period, though not necessarily indicating continuity. Castle Hill at Newhaven has revealed Iron Age and Roman finds. Also Chyngton at Seaford has evidence of a Roman farmstead. The Caburn, a chalk hill ringed with circular earth works and ditches from the Iron Age period, and peppered within with 150 pits, commands the Lower Ouse, The Levels and surrounding downland. Barrows and cross dykes scatter the downland around the river valley.

The Roman presence is not demonstrated by military forts but by farmsteads and country villas. Two villa/farmsteads, north of the Downs, at Beddingham/Preston and Barcombe (ongoing 2001-2006) have been excavated. Another excavated site lies under the Police Station, ring road and car park at Newhaven. Of the 1st and 2nd century the function of the site suggests preparation for the export of salted beef, hides, meats and other produce from the hinterland[3]. Highdole, a Romano-British site up in the downland west of Rodmell, appears to have had an outlying pastoral function for raising cattle and sheep. Part of a Romano-British site at Ranscombe Hill was unearthed in 1976 when the A27 was widened.[4]

Evidence of the early Saxon presence is very tentative. The 6th century pagan Saxon cemetry at Saxonbury near Southover has already been mentioned. There is another extensive Saxon burial area sited on the shoulder of Chalk below Malling Down, to the east opposite the promontory on which Lewes (OE *laew* – 'slope or barrows') developed from the Saxon defensive burh constructed by King Alfred c.AD900. A sunken floored building of early to mid Saxon date has recently been unearthed on the low valley side just north of the present site of Itford farm. There are other known Saxon burial sites near Preston Court (Beddingham) and notably at Loover Hill by Glynde Reach. A part-burial site was reported in 1852 alongside the cemetry wall of Southease church. Recent excavations east of the main river valley at Bishopstone, 2002-2006, under the direction of Sussex Archaeological Society's former research officer G. Thomas, has proved to be a spectacular site of a late Saxon 9/10th century period. A complex settlement was revealed immediately north of the churchyard and the Saxon church, with post holes for substantial timber structures, burials and pits, providing one of the largest assemblages for this period found in the south of England[5].

All around on downland slopes field systems of small rectangular and square dimensions have been noticed and recorded.

They appear on Malling Down to Saxon Down and on The Caburn. Much of the downland has been and is extensively ploughed, but the steeper slopes can still reveal former field systems. A spread of square fields and track ways has been noted and drawn from aerial photographs of an area on the slopes behind Tarring Neville.

Field names on 17th and 18th century maps recording 'The Comp' provide a potential indication of Roman estates in the area, also included could be furlong names such as Stoneland and Greystone furlongs (e.g. at Kingston). This OE *comp*, a borrowing from the Latin *campus* appears to mean 'land on the edge of a villa estate', and R. Coates (1990) suggested that the word could have applied to neglected arable land with the junction of marshland/brookland. At Beddingham there is Comp Wish – OE *wisc* 'marshy meadow', – the use of the word was used extensively in Sussex. Perhaps it is significant that both areas were later Saxon royal estates as previously mentioned, and taken over after the Conquest by Normans of high status[6].

Place Names

All the settlement names indicate land that had been cleared of woodland by the period in which settlements became named. Topographic type names are considered to be early in the chronology of Old English i.e. Saxon, later habitive names are from the 7th century onwards. Topographic type names in the valley are –over, –ford, –hoe, –dene, –ease, –mell, –ham. Later habitive names are the three *tun* names of Sutton, Norton and Kingston, indicative of inclusive settlements of the royal multiple Saxon estate of Iford (*eg* + *ford* – 'ford to the island'). By the later Saxon period just before the Conquest, Iford was held by Queen Edith, wife of King Edward and Earl Godwin's sister.

The other *tun* names are situated in the south east area of the Lower Ouse, – Bishopstone, Denton, South Heighton, Sutton and East Blatchington, and again it could be suggested they are land holdings derived from a Saxon estate. Bishopstone was probably a new naming when the landholding was endowed to the bishops of

Chichester by the 9th century. Also South Heighton with Southease and Telscombe were 10th century endowments to the Abbey of Hyde at Winchester. The charter of King Edgar dated AD 966, grants the church of Southease with 28 hides of land and the church of Telscombe with 10 hides of land[7].

Beddingham (OE *hamm*, 'low promontory surrounded by marsh/water') was the settlement of Beadas people and has been ascribed with a church of minister status. A royal manor of King Edward, the manor was obliged to pay 'one night's revenue' for an itinerant king's visitation. Southerham was a manorial holding of the Archbishop of Canterbury's large estate of South Malling. A new perspective by G. Vines and F. Price (SAC 143, 2005) presents Southerham through a long period of use[8].

The early Medieval period

All this low lying brookland has a long history as a valuable resource for the villagers and landholders who worked the land and lived in settlements on the east and west sides. The earliest documented evidence of drainage and meadow comes from a 10th century charter (AD957) for South Heighton, which describes the boundaries of the landholding given as an endowment to the New Minister at Winchester. The itinerary starts at the river, then along the fleet and then the (ME) *ditch* to (ME) *hokclyve*. The boundary extended up to high point on the downland at Five Lords Burgh before returning to the brookland then to the river, forming a typical combination of resources for a linear parish[9]. These long linear landholdings which became incorporated into parishes lying east to west, extended one after the other along the Lower Ouse valley, with a habitat made of downland pasture, light loam soils at the scarpfoot and lower slopes, and marshland which provide drained brookland for hay meadows and summer grazing.

Orientated at right angles to the river valley are a sequence of tracks, droveways and hedgelines extending for 5-6 km from a high points or watersheds between coombes. These east and west divisions suggest landholdings demarcated for the exploitation of grazing and movements of beasts to and from core settlements sited on spring lines between the marsh/brooklands and the higher pastures. It is thought that these 'co-axial landscapes' could be of early origin (Bronze Age) and subsequent field systems have utilised the landscape but the linear element has remained[10].

Salterns and Marshland

Due to the tidal ebb and flow in the earlier period, salt extraction and fisheries were important resources. In the Domesday Survey of 1086, 11 salthouses were recorded in the manor of Rodmell (OE *red + melde* 'red earth'). Briney mud silt was boiled to extract the salt and during the process a red bricquetage built up residues to form low extensive mounds no longer evident in the Ouse valley, but which can still be found in the Adur valley and Pevensey Marshes. Southease and Northease, lying to the south and north of Rodmell grew brushwood crops (OE *haes* 'brushwood') to provide fuel for the boiling process[11].

At Beddingham 4 salthouses were recorded, and further up Glynde Reach in the area of Laughton Levels there were 16 salthouses. However, it should be noted that the lands of the manor of Laughton outreached to other landholdings in the Rape of Pevensey, so that the siting of the salthouses could be elsewhere e.g. Pevensey marshes. Other salterns were probable in the saltmarshes of the river estuary from Denton to Seaford. The record of these salthouses at this late 11th century date could indicate a vigorous pattern of tidal flows into perhaps controlled areas in order that salty silts could settle.

Meadows

The Domesday record of 1086 notates acres of meadows attached to the vills of the Lower Ouse, and does not give the impression of a flooded valley. On the west side, the meadowland was extensive suggesting that marsh land had been artificially drained to some extent. At Iford which included Kingston, Swanborough and

Northease, there were 208 acres of meadow. At Rodmell there were 140 acres and the 11 salthouses. At *Orleswick* near Piddinghoe there were 17 acres and also 17 acres at *Harpingden* (Deans). At Southease, the holding of the Abbey of Hyde, Winchester, there were 130 acres.

On the east side, Beddingham was recorded with 50 acres and the 4 salthouses, and Itford had 50 acres. Tarring Neville, adjacent to South Heighton where the entry does not record any meadow acreage, had again 50 acres. West Firle had 72 acres of meadow lying along Glynde Reach in Laughton Levels. Meadows at Southerham and Ranscombe were included in the 200 acres of meadowland of the large manor of South Malling, held by the Archbishop of Canterbury. Hamsey, north of Lewes, had 200 acres of meadow lying on the west bank of the river Ouse. From Rodmell to Meeching there are a series of bottoms leading off from the low river valley floor which would have been affected by tidal water from time to time in the earlier period. The topographic term of bottom, OE *botm* can be applied to these features with flat low wet land with abrupt steep valley sides, which could have been dammed and ditched to provide meadows for hay and summer grazing, *Orleswick* and *Harpingden* both had 17 acres of meadow probably in the bottom of the combes[12].

The Medieval Period

After the Norman Conquest the composite estates of the Saxon aristocracy were redistributed into Norman lordships. The policy of the new lords was estate improvement, which included open fields and planned villages, new stone built churches and castles, the foundation of boroughs with markets and fairs. From the latter part of the 11th century onwards more and more endowments of land and property enhanced the wealth of Norman monastic foundations. Capitalised and with administrative expertise, ecclesiastical estates became extensive. An example of an endowment was the demesne landholding at Swanborough of 6½ hides later added to, which amounted to an 800 acre (340 ha) grange farm with a stone built hall. The Norman monastic estates also had the benefit of expertise

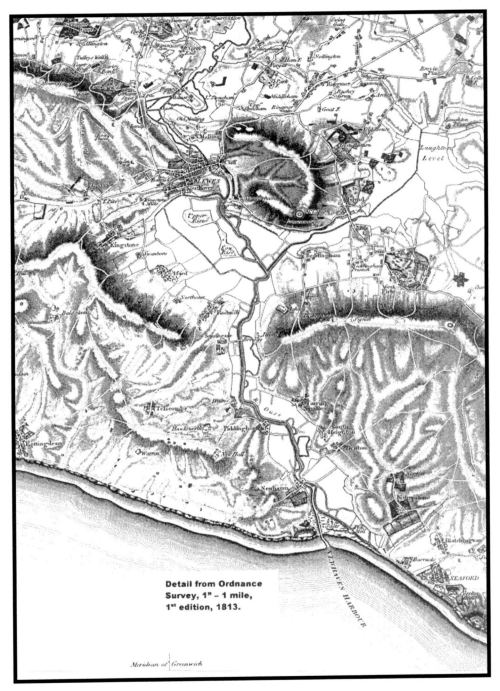

**Detail from Ordnance
Survey, 1" – 1 mile,
1st edition, 1813.**

Meridian of Greenwich

*Fig 2: Lewes to Newhaven,
detail from 1813 ordnance survey*

of hydraulic water systems based on the mother abbeys in Europe. A key part to improvements was progressing drainage to form meadows able to support increased stocks of cattle and sheep[13].

Battle Abbey's documents provide evidence of dykes and sea walls being constructed to reclaim land below Barnhorne at Pevensey Levels from 1107-1124. A little later, 12th – 13th century, the ecclesiastical estates of Michelham Priory and Ashburnham reclaimed areas to the north and the west, for freshwater pastures. Further east in Romney Marsh, B. Cunliffe's excavations at Stutfall near Lympne, provided evidence of Roman reclamation of salt marsh[14].

At Lewes, the Priory of St Pancras founded in 1077 by Earl William de Warenne and his wife Gundrada, was located on the probable site of a previous Saxon minster church. The site on a low Chalk promontory 5m OD at Southover, lying below Lewes Castle, extended over nearly 40 acres (24 ha) with the Winterbourne stream to the north and the Cockshut stream on the south. A levelled watercourse diverted from the feeder sources of the Cockshut stream provided water for a reservoir at the *Pada Pool*, supplying water for the mill, fish ponds, kitchens and reredorters. The main stream was tidal to just below the monastic site. The Priory overlooked the extensive alluvial levels to the south, with the two Rises. Land granted to the Priory included 'the island which is nearest to the monastery with meadows and grazing land belonging to it (c.1095) and 'the island which is called Sutheye ... which lies beside the island of the said monks'. The promontory was perceived or translated as an island, as it was in practice, lying on a Chalk spur between two streams and ending at the main river to the east[15].

The problems of periodic flooding on these low lands meant that there had to be an acceptance between landholders, for an understanding of co-operation in order to maintain the walls and dykes. The close relationship of the working of mills, dykes, walls, ditches, sluices, stanks (ME 'a dam to hold water back'), inevitably led to disputes, claims to rights and ultimately to legal statutes. In 1160 it is recorded that Richard Porter of Pevensey granted William, the Prior of St Pancras, Lewes, the right for the ebb and flow of the sea water to pass freely over his marshland at Langney to work the Prior's tide mill there. He, Richard Porter and his wife, were also paid 1 mark of silver and 3 marks of gold and the privilege of having their corn ground first at the mill, – all for the value of the vital movement of the tidal flow[16].

A case of 'some importance' was held in the Michaelmas Term 1202 (*Curia Regis Rolls* 1199 – 1230) when King John ordered the justices to postpone on appeal between the men of William de Warenne II and Hugh de Folkinton, as he wished to hear the case. The court hearing was concerned with the maintenance of dykes in the Ouse valley between Lewes and Seaford. The case was eventually heard in the Easter Term 1204: the Archbishop of Canterbury was uneasy about his rights and had charged a number of defendants for having raised river walls to his nuisance (affecting his fishing at Broadwater, Southerham). One defendant was released and the others failed to appear. At the same time the Archbishop and Prior of Lewes were taking similar actions against Robert de Denton and Robert de Marci. The latter 'put himself' on the Archbishop's men of South Malling and on the Earl de Warenne's men of Piddinghoe and Meeching, 'by whom the walls were mended as they ought to be'[17].

Marsh walls were 'a near approach to public works', and custom and law of the marsh was recorded prior to 1210-1240. It was after the Great Flood of 1287 when the sea had broken walls and caused great damage, that two years later is the first record (c.1292) of the Commissioners of Sewers for the Sussex Coast. Thereafter Commissioners became a regular controlling group or Watercourt for each particular Level. Few earlier reports have survived. However, the statutes of the Marshes of Pevensey and Romney (1402) were subsequently bequeathed to the Ashmolean Museum, in Oxford by Sir William Dugdale, which had been loaned to him when he collected material for his book 'Imbanking and Drainage of the Country' written in 1772 (*SAC* 18, [1867]). Romney marsh had more ancient customs and rights than Pevensey Levels and the Pevensey statutes were based on them as were those of the Ouse valley. Dugdale writes that between 1289-1398 a multitude of Commissions were granted 'for the view and care of banks and ditches of various marshes in Sussex'[18].

Late Medieval and Tudor Drainage

In the year 1421 (9 Hen V) a Commission of Sewers was granted to inspect and repair the banks of The Levels through which the river Ouse runs from Fletching to Seaford. Eleven commissioners named from the principal landowners in the area included Thomas Nelond, Prior of Lewes and Sir John Pelham of Laughton. By this period the custom and laws of maintenance of the drainage were well established and based on the 'ancient laws' of Pevensey Marshes, of the time of Henry III 1258 which were recited in the later volumes of the Commission of Sewers for Lewes and Laughton Levels from 1626 to 1950. Further acts for Commission of Sewers through the 15th century reflected 'the excessive rising of waters of that period'. The precious hay meadows were frequently covered with standing water during the summer months. Adjacent to Glynde Reach at West Firle the tenantry of the shared meadow land, 1st, 2nd, 3rd *weders*, were drawn by lots and marked by *pawls*. In 1469 the occupiers were subject to penalty fines 'if they do not clean out their ditches and watercourses, nor keep them in order as they should'.

In 1531/2, Henry VIII's Reformation Parliament passed a statute 'to rectify neglect of waterways, sea defences and to repair ruinous bridges' (23 Hen 8). Thereafter the Commission of Sewers had powers to assess, tax and to levy sanctions on those who were liable for the maintenance of the waterways and bridges. They were also empowered to commandeer materials and resources, and also to requisition local workmen, to ensure repairs and maintenance were carried out as required. In 1534 a Commission for the whole of Sussex was appointed consisting of fifty-four landowners of substance, including the Prior of Lewes, Robert Crowham, other Sussex Priors, the Abbot of Battle, the Bishop of Chichester, the Lords of Abergavenny, and de la Warr, Sir John Gage, Sir William Pelham and many significant gentry such as Sackville, Shurley, Fines, Shelley, Michell of Kingston, Chamber of Rodmell.

Fourteen members from the original list were appointed to the Commission for Lewes and Laughton Levels. Sir Henry Ellis's article included the letter from Sir John Gage to Thomas Cromwell

1537, where he related that the Prior of Lewes, himself, went to see and learn from the experienced operators of drainage and water systems in the low lying lands in Flanders and brought back two experts. At this time an order was made for the opening of the mouth of the haven at Meeching, subsequently renamed New Haven. The decision to make this cut through to the sea 'was a carefully conceived plan to improve drainage and also the navigation of the Ouse,' (P.F. Brandon).

Part of a workaday notebook of 1537 lists the names of the occupiers , parish by parish, due to pay the levy on their brookland acreage in order to pay for the new cut for the Haven at Newhaven (Meeching). The notebook lists all the parishes along the Ouse which would benefit from the new harbour exit and consequent better transportation and trade – Iford (Abergaveny), Swanborough (Buckhurst), Rodmell, Plumpton, Barcombe, Newick, Ranscombe, 'Rype', 'Furles', Glynde (Morley), Beddingham, Denton, Southease, Piddinghoe, Northease, Stuckle (Stempe), Kingston and Meeching (Norfolk).

Efforts for general improvements for all the Ouse environment are reflected in an entry (1595) concerning Bishop Sherborne's landholdings at Heighton, Denton and Meeching. A piece of marsh-land, Penner's Eye, 'was wasted by the sea for want of building up the wall. The farmer promises to build up the wall if the adjacent tenants build up theirs.' [19]

In Lewes, meetings of the Watercourt were duly held, and arrangements put in place to levy scots at certain rates per acre on every owner of land in each parish to ensure that the river flowed but also, that the sewers were cleaned in order that the lands were well-drained with fresh water.

Cliffe and Lewes

Cliffe, below Lewes on the low ground formed of deposits of silts and mud, lies on a physically critical but important site, where the river flows through the Chalk escarpment. The source of the principal tributary of the Ouse lies to the north at Plummers Plain in the High Weald. The river develops from a multitude of streams as it flows south to the Low Weald, joined by the river Uck at Isfield and becomes tidal at Barcombe Mills. At Cliffe it is a significant river with a tidal fall and rise of 4-6 metres. The Ouse similar to other Sussex rivers The Cuckmere, Adur and Arun, developed on the south slopes of the Wealden anticline 20-25 million years ago, and subsequently adjusted to the folds and uplifts of the Alpine disturbance during the Pliocene epoch. To the east of the Caburn downland lies Glynde Reach, formerly a tidal branch of the Ouse, which presents as a 'misfit' river, i.e. a small sized river in relation to its environment, lying in the syncline between Caburn and Beddingham hill[20].

Immediately to the east of the river at Cliffe (*OE clif*) the steepness of the slope and exposed Chalk cliff enhanced by 18th to 20th century quarrying, makes the place name particularly appropriate. Early settlement was probably along the base of the cliff just above flood level at 5 metres with springs and wells providing fresh water.

On a Chalk promontory, half a mile to the north (1 km) the Saxon settlement of Malling (*OE meallingas* – Mealla's people) was sited with known pagan burial grounds, encompassed by the river below. This is where the manorial centre of the Archbishop of Canterbury's Wealden manor was located in the Rape of Pevensey. The Canons of St Michael also had their religious community at Malling.

Lewes itself (*OE laew* – slope or barrows) again is sited on a promontory which slopes down to the bridge at Cliffe. The site was selected in the 10th century by King Alfred as one of several *burhs* in Sussex, for defensive purposes. Manpower and resources came from vills and farmsteads encircling Lewes. The Domesday record of 1086 lists manors with burgess plots and sites in the town, probably reflecting the 10th century burghal hidage. King Edward had 127 burgess plots, the manor of Swanborough 26 burgess plots, the manor of Rodmell 44 sites, and the Archbishop of Canterbury had 21 sites belonging to the manor of Malling in Lewes. Immediately after the Conquest, Lewes Castle became the administrative centre of William de Warenne's fiefdom of the Rape of Lewes. The newly erected castle on its large motte was visible in the landscape for miles around, from the north and from the south, placed centrally in the river gap. By 1077 the foundations of the Cluniac Priory of St Pancras had begun with a wealth of endowments[21].

Cliffe and early development

It is likely that Cliffe developed on a chalk causeway made across drained brookland of the manor of Malling. A record for repairs dated 1159 provides evidence for a bridge crossing the river to Lewes. In the Customary of the Archbishop of Canterbury dated 1285, 38 messuages with curtilages and several shops are recorded in Cliffe. It is evident that the settlement was by this period operating as a trading centre based on the causeway and riverside wharves, which eventually became known as West Street and now Cliffe High Street. The advantages of the site connecting routeways to the bridge and Lewes and also to the sea-trade of the river, outweighed the difficulties of the marshy ground and flood episodes. Archaeological excavations (Rudling, 1991) revealed 'made ground' of pounded chalk at Fair Place on the north side of the church of St Thomas à Beckett, providing dry ground for market activities of the 13th and 14th centuries. Grants for weekly markets and two fairs a year were granted by charter in 1409 by the Archbishop and focused trading activities from the Wealden hinterland and immediate downland vicinity[22].

The question arises as to how and why a medieval settlement on a causeway across a flood plain, with a bridge over a tidal river, maintained its position as a successful trading centre, persisting to the present time? The vexed problem of vicarious flooding was a constant anxiety. The slow fall of the river southwards across The Levels to sea level with added silting, enhanced the problem. At some stage, problems at Cliffe had been cleverly resolved by constructing five sewers made of open three-foot wide shallow water channels from north to south, off the main river, able to flush through twice a day, and which helped exit excess floodwater from the river. It proved to be a good solution, but needed regular maintenance, and was linked to problems of the flow of the river and the need of effective drainage from Malling Brooks to the north and the extensive Levels to the south.

Drainage, sewers and The Levels

It was a constant battle to maintain the drainage of The Levels and essential for the ditches, dykes and sluices to be well maintained. Much had been achieved by the time the minute books were being written for the Commission of Sewers starting in 1626 and ending in 1950, when its functions were reorganised and became the Sussex River Board, now the Environment Agency. From the minutes of the regular meetings of the Watercourt can be traced the vicissitudes of the weather and the troublesome problems of flood water, either from the head waters of the river and/or exceptional tides[23]. John de Ward's map dated 1620 shows in place drainage improvements of the river and adjacent lands. The minute books all through 1600-1700 record phrases such as 'sewer stopped', 'water doth not go', 'in decay for want of shoresetting and widening', 'needs cleansing', 'casting and cleansing' and requires to be 'raft and drawn'. In 1645 'the way and wall' from Southover to Pull Barr needed clearing and was in default. In the same year White Wall at Southease 'needed to be heightened'. By 1664 another more successful scheme had improved the mouth of the river at Newhaven. This time merchants and masters of barques and shipping carried the levy, and 'no ballast was to be thrown into the Channel'. In 1695 the Earl of Dorset's sewer at Southover was in great default. The Great Sewer from Shine (Rodmell) to Kingston needed to be shovelled and repaired by adjoining landowners who were levied at a 6d scot per acre.

The 'rage and violence of a great storm' in 1728 caused extensive breaches of walls and floods, causing damage and hurt. 'The Brookland lying within the parish of All Saints, Lewes has been destroyed'. All the efforts of occupiers, landowners and merchants were effecting increasing productivity from land resources. The maps of this period show the brooklands drained with a system of sewers and ditches. At Northease three substantial walls (causeways and adjacent dykes) extended across to Lower Rise, preventing any floodwater reaching the parcelled brookland in between and remain so in present time. White Wall at Southease, and Rodmell functioned in a similar fashion. A great long sewer cut straight through brookland from Kingston to Rodmell, now called 'Celery sewer'[24].

Cliffe and its sewers

In Cliffe the head sewer lay east to west on the north side of the causeway and was integrated with the main river, which was tidal. From here the water fed through a series of five sewers running north to south in open water courses, about three feet wide, past yards, gardens, properties and workshops, dwellings, shops, ale houses, through an arched sewer under the High Street, and southwards to join the main river as it bends round to Southerham, and eventually to the sea at Newhaven. The five sewers from east to west measured 80 rods, 44 rods, 50 rods, 20 rods and 50 rods (16½ feet per rod).

The first entry in 1626 records Cliffe sewers as stopped and filled up and in need of cleansing by a fixed date and, if not, a fine would be levied. Twenty years later the sewers between the Red Lion and the House of Correction were 'in default'. Again, most of the sewers, nine years on, were blocked so that 'the current and passage of the water was affecting the low ground'.

At regular intervals owners/occupiers with land and property adjacent to the sewers were named with lists of rods at a fine per rod for failing to do the maintenance. The formula was for specific tasks such as cleansing, casting (to shovel out), rafting (to remove a floating mass of vegetation, logs, etc.), drawing (to remove obstructions by dragging out), and shoresetting (using props and stakes to reinforce the banks). Willows were reported growing in one of the sewers in 1682 and 'with posts standing in', and were ordered 'to be cut and taken away' as 'causing hindrance and stoppage'. The Great Sewer was reported to be 'very foul and chocked'. All through the last twenty years of the 17th century the sewers were frequently reported at the Watercourts to be in need of attention.

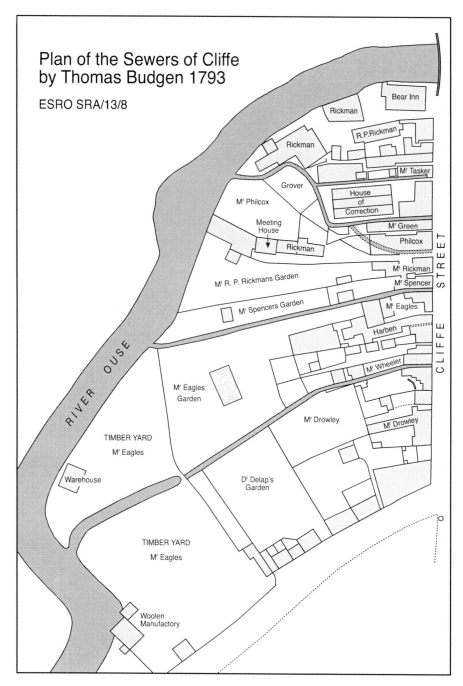

Plan of the Sewers of Cliffe
by Thomas Budgen 1793

ESRO SRA/13/8

Bear Inn

Rickman

R.P.Rickman

Rickman

Mr Tasker

Grover

Mr Philcox

House
of
Correction

Meeting
House

Mr Green

Philcox

Rickman

Mr Rickman

Mr Spencer

Mr R. P. Rickmans Garden

Mr Spencers Garden

Mr Eagles

Harben

RIVER OUSE

Mr Wheeler

Mr Eagles
Garden

Mr Drowley

Mr Drowley

TIMBER YARD

Mr Eagles

Warehouse

Dr Delap's
Garden

TIMBER YARD

Mr Eagles

CLIFFE STREET

Woolen
Manufactory

Fig 3

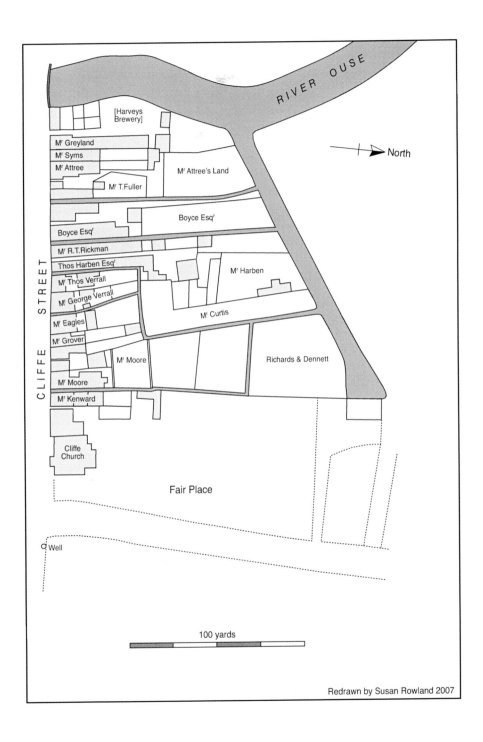

RIVER OUSE

[Harveys Brewery]

Mr Greyland

Mr Syms

Mr Attree

Mr T.Fuller

Mr Attree's Land

Boyce Esqr

Boyce Esqr

Mr R.T.Rickman

Thos Harben Esqr

Mr Thos Verrall

Mr George Verrall

Mr Harben

Mr Curtis

Mr Eagles

Mr Grover

Mr Moore

Richards & Dennett

Mr Moore

Mr Kenward

CLIFFE STREET

Cliffe Church

Fair Place

Well

North

100 yards

Redrawn by Susan Rowland 2007

Lewes bridge had been swept away by a high tide in 1726, and the present bridge is from the rebuild and design of N. Dubois and A. Morris, stonemason, 1727. John Marchant wrote in his diary, 19 November 1727, 'We had a vestry about a fresh demand of 30 and odd pounds towards Lewes Bridge, by a order of Sessions. Never were people more heartily curst all the country over, and never did any better deserve to be so. For I think it cost about as much once before'.

It was reported to the Watercourt 'that the rage and violence of the floods had damaged and swept away Lewes Bridge, the banks of the river had been breached and the low ground in The Levels was submerged.' The jurors of the Watercourt viewed the five sewers that ran through Cliffe and 'found them very much out of repair'. In this year of 1731 there were also 'several props to houses and trees blocking the sewers, which ought to be removed', and there was also 'filth and rubbish'. A fine of 4 shillings per rod was levied by the Watercourt on the owners and occupiers of adjacent properties, to be paid by a fixed date that year.

However, the problems of flooding continued to be severe in the 18th century. The proposal was to build lockgates on land purchased at Denton, in order to reduce the impact of spring tides on the river flow, which was held upstream during these periods. Public consultation took place on 29 January 1732 at two o'clock, so that 'any persons with objections may appear'. Public notices were placed in Seaford, Newhaven and Lewes about the propsals.

At the next Watercourt in 1732 John Joliffe Esq. of Denton was paid £5 for land 'taken off' for the lock or floodgates. It was agreed that the gates would only be shut during the months of March, April, May, June, July, August and September yearly, and 'they be shut constantly every year the first and second days after the New and Full Moon, within the month of March and April, and at other times only as the Waterbailiff thinks convenient'. Public notices announcing the times would be shown at Lewes and Newhaven.

The lockgates were duly constructed, but three years later there was an order for payment of repairs. The next year, 1736, there was an order for pulling down the lockgates as not repairable. The lockgates were to be cut off at the sides, and all timber 'as such as can be found scattered abroad on The Levels' and also any persons 'who had taken away any of the broken timber' were to be reported to the Waterbailiff, and prosecuted at the next Court.

In 1742 the five sewers in Cliffe were reported to be 'in default and decay and needing cleansing', and occupiers were ordered to carry out the work by 1 August. A similar order was placed on the contiguous owners/occupiers of the five sewers in 1751. It appears that work was not done, because in the following year the Waterbailiff collected money to pay for the work at 8s. per rod. From May to November 1752, 129 days of labour were paid for the cleaning and repairs of the sewers at a cost of £81.06d. and £4.12s. for beer[25].

The Eighteenth Century and Engineering

The 'Main River' at this time was very sluggish, with the tidal flow hardly reaching Lewes Bridge. The Watercourt records obstructions of reeds, flags and other weeds growing and encroaching on shores and on banks that had fallen into the river. None of these conditions could have made the Cliffe sewers flow or be cleansed by daily tides.

The Commission of Sewers again sought professional expertise, and Mr John Smeaton, engineer, was commissioned and all the commissioners duly received his report, and each had a plan drawn by John Marchant, for consideration. They met and duly adjourned the meeting to the White Hart at 10 o'clock, 2 January 1769. Another meeting was adjourned, and eventually in June of that year it was agreed that the Waterbailiff and selected jurors were to view the river from Cliffe Bridge to Newhaven on 28 June 1769, and also from Barcombe Mill to said Bridge on another agreed day, 'for the more speedy carrying off the Tides and Floods'.

Mr Smeaton's Report on Lewes and Laughton Level dated 1768 would have given the Commissioners plenty of information for debate. They already knew that the water flow of the river and the problems of incoming high spring tides often caused serious flooding. Mr Smeaton measured the levels of the tides and where they reached the different parts of the river. He noticed that banks were not high enough and outfalls of sluices were not low enough. The river was too crooked and obstructions narrowed the flow and 'the natural declivity of the river is small'. He produced two methods to deal with these problems. One – was to straighten the river, and to shut out the tides flowing up the river, to have gates or sluices, and to discharge fresh water through outfall sluices, and to embank east and west sides of the river with drainage aided by sluices. Two – the river was to remain as it was, to embank low land and to convey flood water by a separate canal or sewer 12 foot in diameter with sluices at outfalls to prevent 'reflux of Tides'. It included subterraneous tunnels with branches across The Levels to fall in with Kingston drain, and a north branch to pass between the two Rises. Also to bring down the Cockshut Water 'which will be useful for cattle', through Lewes Brooks and in 'a subterranean tunnel' under the river Ouse and then 'answerable to one of the old passages that cross the street east of Lewes Bridge (i.e. Cliffe), from thence to Malling Brooks and again 'cross the river into Lewes Brooks and up to Landport Brooks'. Costs were considerable – £10,000 for the first scheme, £9,000 for the second. Ultimately the second method was discarded and the first developed slowly in stages[26]. However, the problem of the flow of the main river was still under consideration. All the Commissioners were major landowners and entrepreneurs as well as agriculturists. Particularly active were Thomas Pelham of Stanmer Park, 2nd Earl of Chichester, and John Baker Holroyd of Sheffield, 1st Earl of Sheffield[27.]

In 1787 the Rt. Hon. Thomas Pelham was corresponding from Stanmer House with Mr Jessop, engineer, about the improvement of the navigation of the river Ouse. Mr Jessop wrote that he agreed with Mr Smeaton's report, and some of the improvements carried out since 1768 had been effective. For navigation in the main river there were still too many obstructions and shallows, and at Southease the river was narrow, crooked and shallow, so that barges drawing only two feet got 'fast' at neap tides. So he recommended that it be widened and straightened, and also to remove the banks 'further into the land' and make a new cut across Southease brooks, setting the banks 30 feet each side. The banks above White Wall (Southease)

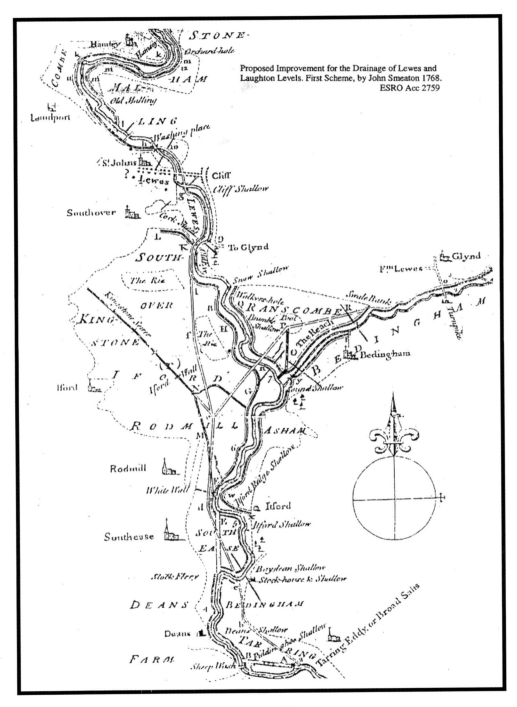

Proposed Improvement for the Drainage of Lewes and
Laughton Levels. First Scheme, by John Smeaton 1768.
ESRO Acc 2759

*Fig 4: Proposed improvement for drainage of Lewes and
Laughton Levels by J. Smeaton 1768*

were to be raised to accommodate the flow of the tidal water, and barges drawing four feet would be able to pass up the river at neap tides. Landowners of the low grounds would need to lower their sluices as all were too high to discharge floodwater effectively. A horse-towing path was recommended from Lewes to Piddinghoe. Pelham, aware of pressures likely to come from landowners and traders, raised the question of who should pay, and Jessop responded that both should pay because the wider cuts would make trade more viable. And he added that extending the navigation beyond Cliffe/ Lewes to Barcombe Mill would be very practical, but would need a lock at Hamsey.

Work on straightening the river on the meanders at Baydean and the bends in general from White Wall north of Southease southwards to Deans and Piddinghoe were carried out between 1774 and 1779. Men were paid 3d. for a yard's work, which included bottoming, casting back, and loading barges. Luke Spence, Waterbailiff for the Commission, paid £867 for this river work including the beer[28].

Persons interested in the Trade and Navigation of the river Ouse from Newhaven to Barcombe Mill were invited to attend a meeting at the Bridge Coffee House on 28 November 1789. The objective was to agree an application to Parliament for an Act to improve the navigation. In 1793 Thomas Budgen surveyed and produced the plan of Cliffe sewers but also of other areas of Lewes and Laughton Levels. The Act was approved in June 1794. A separate river scot was now able to be levied at varying rates according to the benefits to be gained by traders and by adjoining landowners/occupiers. The river environment was divided into five districts:-

First District	Newhaven Bridge to Stock Ferry
Second District	Stock Ferry to Cliffe Bridge
Third District	Lewes Bridge to Bushey Brook
Fourth District	Hamsey Bridge to Barcombe Mill
Fifth District	Laughton Levels

The feasibility surveys of Smeaton in 1767 and a further report by the engineer Jessop in 1787 identified the problem of the

Celery sewer across The Levels and Itford hill in the distance

Flooded "bottom" in combe at Deans

Lewes Bridge to Cliffe High Street

Bridge rebuilt from design of N. Dubois, 1727

The Shine, embanked river and Caburn

Sweeping bend of the river, Piddinghoe

The Ouse at Cliffe and former warehouses

The Ouse north of the bridge and recent raised wall of the brewery

Rodmell sluice at end of Celery sewer

Rodmell sluice and ancillary sluice exiting into the river

Cattle grazing

Drainage ditch trampled and in need of 'casting and cleansing'

*The Levels, Upper Rise centre left, and the Downs
above Kingston and Swanborough*

*Thirty feet width from the river bank, now much heightened.
Cliffe in the distance.*

The River Ouse passing under Southease Bridge and 'shoresetting'

Lewes Flood, 12 October 2000

slight gradient of the Lower Ouse and associated flooding. Their solution was to tackle the whole area as an entity and not in a 'piecemeal fashion'. The result was the Lower Ouse Navigation Act 1791 which enabled capital to be raised, engineering works to be done at Newhaven to stabilise the entrance, and slow sweeping bends and meanders were blocked off, embankments raised and the river widened and dredged. The effect was to speed up the flow, so that a navigable channel was achieved and also the drainage of the brookland assisted. Another important effect was to give a better tidal rise and fall up to Cliffe and Lewes and beyond. Prior to 1790 it had only been barely 1 foot (16cm). Tidal variation now became as much as 11 feet (3.40metres) at spring tides. Wharves and warehouses on the banks at Cliffe and Lewes could now be serviced by barges from the improved port at Newhaven[29]. The acreage of the Second District, which included the parishes of Tarring Neville, Beddingham, Glynde, Ranscombe, Cliffe, Southover, Kingston, Iford, Rodmell and Southease amounted to 2,099 acres. The grand total for all five districts of the Levels was 4,716 acres. But by 1794 several cross sewers under Cliffe High Street were again so badly obstructed that John Ellman, Waterbailiff, received a payment for the expense of moving these obstructions. Two years later, 1796, the eastern sewer 'had been lately stopped up'. By the next year, the Watercourt records new sluices on several low lands lying on the east side of the river to Malling Brooks to the north and to a wharf adjoining the Cliffe Great Sewer, consisting of 5 acres belonging to Mr Whitfield, and it was agreed that £5 was to be raised for a 'new Trunk' (i.e. branch for extra wharf space). Navigation on the improved river flow produced more barge activity, but 'rafts' of timber moored in the main river caused hindrance to river transportation. Improvements to drains, sluices and banks were ongoing.

Agricultural achievement from the 17th century to the 19th century

The relationship of the brookland to the arable land along with the downland pasture functioned as a sustainable agrarian system over many centuries. By the 17th century, adaptations developed principally to crops and stock and to land tenure. By the 18th and 19th centuries changes responding to the demands of population growth became so evident that the period has been deemed the 'agricultural revolution' although writers like Overton (2001) describe the change as 'a transformation'. Small amounts of yardlands for arable crops with associated rights to fallow and pasture shifted from copyholders into the ownership of larger landholders. Often when the copyholds came to the end of their lives before the manorial court, they would be enfranchised and became, in effect, freeholds. Engrossment and capital investment enhanced estates with improved buildings, dwellings, stock and new introductions of seed, turnips and grass leys. Input of capital and confidence resulted in canal building, turnpike roads and shipping to overseas markets. Market possibilities were reflected in the south-east by the 'London-derived' growth and expansion. [30].

In Sussex the large landowners had always been to the forefront of capitalising their estates. John Baker Holroyd (1st Earl of Sheffield) built a model farm, a landscape park and improved acres of farmland at Sheffield Park near to the river Ouse, north of Lewes. The Gages at Firle, the Morleys (Trevors) at Glynde rebuilt and improved, also Lord Pelham at Bishopstone, though the house was used as a hunting lodge, but all effected improvements[31]. In the Lower Ouse valley the engrossing tenant farmers, Thomas Rogers at Kingston, John Rogers at Swanborough, the Saxbys at Rodmell, and the Watermans at Piddinghoe were working to a new formula by integrating the arable with animal husbandry. Fallow was no longer part of the four course rotation. There was a switch to rotational legumes and grasses, especially rye grass (leys) with successive sowings of wheat and barley, known as alternative husbandry. The result was a significant recurrent input of nitrogen, reviving soils after centuries of tillage. The efforts of improvers focussed on trying new crops and new seed varieties, not only to produce more wheat, barley and oats, but to grow more fodder crops to improve quicker growth in animals both for meat and for wool. Rough land, heath, overgrown hedges were all regarded as waste and in need of improvement[32]. The Napoleonic wars (1790-1815) heightened demand for a wide range of products.

The Rev. Arthur Young, who wrote 'The General View of Agriculture' (1813) observed and praised changes in Sussex prior to this date. Many of his observations were focussed on the productivity that could be gained from introductions and experiments with new grasses (sainfoin, rye, clover) sown in leys, also tares, coleseed and turnips grown for overwinter fodder for stock. Methods for increasing output per acre were observed, new rotations discussed and undersowing praised (called gratten in Sussex). Fallow was no longer part of the seasonal pattern, nor permanent pasture on the downland. One of the most famous tenant farmers was John Ellman of Glynde (1753-1832), who in the Rev. Young's opinion was able to achieve, through careful husbandry, miraculous weed-free crops and flourishing improved stock. He is especially famed for breeding the improved Southdown sheep, which became renowned world wide, and also the development of the red Sussex cattle. He was also an agricultural educator. John Ellman also tenanted 100 acres of brookland called The Shine, lying in the north-east corner of Rodmell parish, enriched by good drainage. Opposite was Sound Bridge and the entrance to the Reach, where probably the cut hay was transported by water and then carted to Place Farm. A drawn survey by Sylvan Harmer dated 1853 shows The Shine divided by ditches into five large parcels of land, an improvement from the multiple parcels drawn in earlier surveys.

The Rev. Young also reported how Thomas Carr of Beddingham, when tenant of Lord Pelham's farm at Bishopstone, recovered land from the sea, which proved so fertile that it yielded 'six fine crops of wheat in as many years'. He also praised the several thousand acres of marshland 'these marshes are to be ranked the finest of their kind', and 'very considerable improvements have been effected'. Approval was expressed for the conduct of the grazier 'in the management of the fertile Level'. Both sheep, for meat and wool, and cattle could be very profitable, and horses especially in time of war. The improved drainage schemes of the Lewes and Laughton Levels were benefiting graziers, by 'opening and cleansing ditches' and 'making drains at proper times to receive superfluous water' meant that drier brookland could increase the quantity of sheep annually pastured. 'Profit is very considerable' as he demonstrated in the calculations tabled in his book[33].

'Watered meadows' were much approved of, and considered an 'admirable practice'. He describes how the water is let on the grass in December for three weeks. In spring the water is spread at twenty-four hour intervals and in May, it ceases. In July, two to three tons of hay are mown per acre, and then left for cattle grazing until December. The practice was widespread on valley floors of chalkland areas, especially in Dorset, Hampshire and Wiltshire. The Rev. Young describes the practice in the Lavant Valley, north of Chichester. The earliest record is in the court rolls of Alfpudddle, Dorset in 1608. In Sussex in the parish of Kingston there were watered meadows known as 'the Cannells' which were drawn on John de Ward's map of 1620. Designed as a floating water system of 17 acres, the Cockshut stream supplied by springs near the village, flowed all the year long and fed the upper watercourse, which was levelled originally to supply water to the Priory complex of mills, kitchens, reredorters. The water flow was fed through hatches and sluices into shallow troughs between the ½ to 1 acre divisions of meadow and then flowed down into the main stream. The early grass provided fodder for ewes and lambs in March and April, and then, irrigated again, for two hay crops. In Kingston a system of lotting has been recorded, with a rotation over ten years. The customs of lotting and cutting of the hay have also been kept in the records of Southease and of West Firle.

There is also evidence of 'watered' brookland at Rodmell, where divided acres of improved pasture were drained and watered by a fresh water stream with a constant all year flow. In these parishes these valuable meadows were owned and controlled by the principal farmers and, by late 18th century, also by graziers. The existing copyholders had rights to pasture on the tenantry brookland, common pasture, called Hubberds, stated by numbers according to the number of arable yardlands that each held. Some of the best hay meadows were at Southease shared with Telscombe, which as a downland parish had no meadows, and with South Heighton on the east side of the river. Tenantry customs and lotting were recorded in Budgen's plan and formed two articles written by W. Figg in 1850 and 1851 (*SAC* 3 and 4). Associated with work services for the manorial lord was the requirement to provide the reapers, men and women, at harvest time with plentiful bread and cheese, also drink at all times

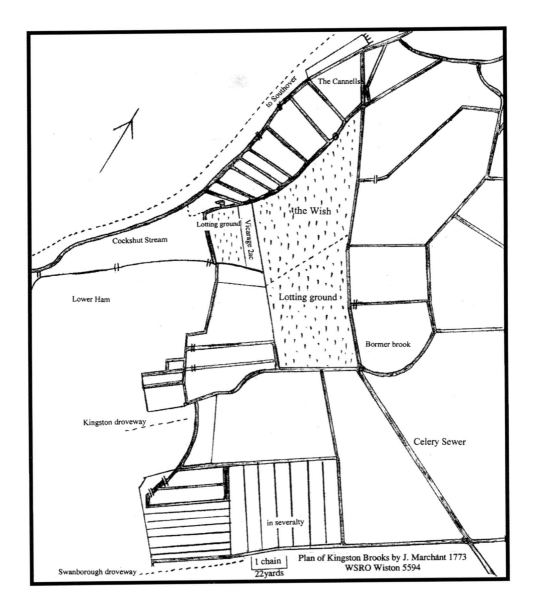

Fig 5: Plan of Kingston Brooks by J. Marchant, 1773

during the day, freely available in the barn. At noon a good meal of roast meat was provided. The tenants from South Heighton crossed at Stock Ferry at a designated time, and had rights to 'cut and carry away' hay from 3½ hides in the North Wish. W. Figg also describes the tradition of the Drinkers' Acre attached to one yardland, which was held by a tenant once in the 10 year rotation of lotting, who paid for 'a drinking'. At Southease a set formula of drawing lots and marking out with sticks divided the hay meadows into hides in North Wish and South Wish and into clouts in Further North Wish and South Wish tenantry grounds. The Drinker Hide was auctioned to the highest bidders and the proceeds spent, presumably on ale. By 1790, plots surrounded by drainage ditches were in individual ownership[34].

Tenantry land in the brookland recorded in Budgen's 1790 plan was as follows: in Kingston there were 115 acres lying in the Wish and Nitch of the Wish; Southover brooklands were held by individual graziers; the 445 acres at Norton and Sutton in Iford parish were held in two parts equally divided by a 17th century reorganisation. Stretching across the brookland to Lower and Upper Rise were walls made of raised embanked chalk causeways, 30 feet wide, with ditches either side. Of the 400 acres at Rodmell, 154 were held by tenantry rights, mainly in the Hubberds. Southease, with especially favourable hay meadows in 237 acres of brookland alongside the river, still had 201 acres held by the tenantry. A small amount of 11 acres remained on the south edge of the parish of Piddinghoe. Meeching and Denton had 200 acres and Tarring provided extensive brookland for graziers held principally by the Rev. Geere, Lord Sheffield and Mr Elphick. The port at Newhaven was nearby for shipping livestock. On the east side some tenantry land existed in Beddingham, there was more in West Firle by Glynde Reach, and none at Southerham[35].

A preliminary plan by T. Budgen (1790) of all the brookland in the Lewes and Laughton Levels was drawn as a preparation for a legal and final plan to level the scot (water tax) by the Commissioners on all the occupiers and owners. The plans provided a survey of the well-drained brooklands and also at this date the reduced remaining areas of tenantry brookland. The only three existing Enclosure Awards are for the parishes of Kingston (1833) and Southease (1836)

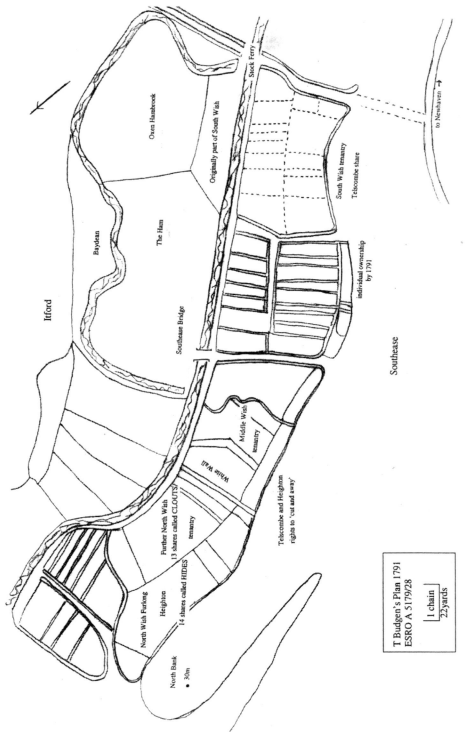

Fig 6: Plan of Southover Brooks by T. Budgen 1791

Itford

Baydean

Oxen Hambrook

The Ham

Originally part of South Wish

Stock Ferry

to Newhaven

South Wish tenanry
Telscombe share

individual ownership
by 1791

Southease Bridge

Southease

White Wall

Middle Wish
tenanry

Telscombe and Heighton
rights to 'cut and away'

Further North Wish
13 shares called CLOUTS
tenanry

North Wish Furlong

Heighton
14 shares called HIDES

North Bank
• 30m

T Budgen's Plan 1791
ESRO A 5179/28

1 chain
22yards

and Telscombe (1810), so at this date of 1790 the old layout and associated lotting is still evident in the plans. Otherwise the evidence points to earlier enclosure by agreement[36].

By the 19th century economic pressure and response culminated in a period of 'high farming'. It was an intensive system of farming with 'high inputs and high outputs'. In the Lower Ouse valley it was based on sheep/corn farming well adapted to the downland, malm soils at the scarpfoot, and brooklands. Wealthy landowners and county families, such as the Trevors of Glynde and Gages of Firle, both with land in Beddingham and Tarring Neville and Southerham, profited from their investments. The Budgen plan of 1790 still reveals piecemeal ownership, but purchases of land and the raising of mortgages from 1810 onwards resulted in consolidation of large estates of 1,000 acres (560 ha) to 2,000 acres (1,200 ha) with high status tenant farmers, comprising two-thirds of the Lower Ouse valley, changing little until the early 20th century[37].

Solving the problem of sewers in Cliffe

River improvements had not solved Cliffe sewers' problems, as by 1814 several cross sewers leading from the Great Sewer on the north side of the High Street to the river on the south were in default and decay 'for want of being cleansed and deepened' and which ought to be done by the owners and occupiers of adjoining properties, 'except such parts of the said sewers as lie under the main road of Cliff'. The Watercourt (1815) gave further consideration to the relationship of the function of the Cliffe sewers with the adjacent low lands, especially those of Malling to the north. So another survey was commissioned. Next year at the June meeting a report was received and consequently Mr Amon Wilds was employed 'to ascertain the Run in the Cliff Sewers from the Archways under the Street to the extremity each way in all of them', and also to assess the capacity for the 'ingress and egress of water'. Samuel Dunstone, Inspector of Sewers, was paid £23.3s. for cleansing the archways under Cliffe Street. Mr Amon Wilds was also ordered to take the section of the river between the Bridge and old Southerham, and to provide information about the practicality of increasing the waterway. Presumably works for improved water depth and flow was accomplished as wharves were extended.

But again in 1822 and 1823 the sewers were in a blocked state. Appeals against the potential fines, and the deadline to carry out the cleansing and moving of obstructions, were made by the notable owners and occupiers of that period – Thomas Hoper, Samuel Flint, John Harvey, Thomas Fuller, Daniel Harvey, Jeremiah Wimble, Benjamin and John Langford, Abraham Curtis, and George Wille. The arguments must have been reasonable, the fault of the flow not theirs, and the Watercourt 'made no order thereon'.

By 1828 the Cliffe Improvement Bill meant the Commissioners were able to approve the application of John Woolgar and Richard Goodyear to arch over the common sewer between their premises, at the same width and height as those under the High Street, but at their own expense.

In 1838 there was stormy weather, and heavy snowfall caused an avalanche down the steep slopes at Cliffe and caused eight deaths. But the cleansing and clearance of obstructions was still an issue in 1838, and the Watercourt adjourned the regular meeting to a further one at the Star Inn in order to receive applications from owners/occupiers of houses and lands 'relative to the cleansing and casting'. In 1845 the sewer from Hillman's brewhouse to the river needed cleansing, and John Harvey's Wharf that formed the river wall on the east side next above Lewes Bridge 'is in default and decay, so the free current of the water is impeded'.

Evidently the arching over of the sewers, depending on individual owners to bear the expense, was piecemeal and not effective. The total length of the five sewers running through Cliffe added up to a total of 3,391 yards, with sixty proprietors liable for scot. In a plan by W. Figg the sewers are shown coloured red and blue, the latter for covered sewers, which amounted to about half at this date. Health problems were often reported, with outbreaks of measles and smallpox. The Commissioners resolved to put into action their powers, designated in the Cliffe Improvement Act (9 Geo.IV, 1828), so that at last in 1849 the open water courses of the five sewers were arched over 'so that the passage be not less than 18 inches in diameter'. Thereafter the sewer system was managed by the Superintendent of Drainage for Cliffe. The Act meant that monies could be levied on the citizens of Cliffe and works put into action for footways to be paved, pipes laid for gas lighting, a clean water pump provided, watchmen at night time, and clearance of obstructions in pathways. Also no filth was allowed to be emptied into the water channels or drains including 'any dead carcass, offal or filth'. For the latter there was a fine of £5. With the five sewers arched over and Cliffe cleaned and lit up, the future for commerce and trade was even more promising.

However, the arching of the sewers did not entirely solve other water problems in Cliffe. The Corporation of Lewes had to seek the expertise of King's Counsel at the turn of the century concerning a problem of river pollution. In his brief Mr A. MacMorrain wrote thus: 'Cliffe was incorporated into the borough of Lewes in 1881. In 1901 the population on the west side of the river was 9,148 and on the east side 2,101, of the population of Lewes lived on chalk and on alluvium. All tides in the river extended to Hamsey and spring tides to Barcombe Mills, and the entire length of the river was washed out regularly by the tides twice every day. Barges navigated the river and sometimes 160-ton burden vessels came to the wharves. Before 1881 the main sewage of Lewes drained into the river, not being subject to treatment, at the outfall at Corporation Wharf at the bottom of North Street. The drainage of the Cliffe side had hitherto been peculiar; at some unknown date certain ditches or culverts, five in number, were constructed in Cliffe. These culverts were probably constructed by the Commission of Sewers of Lewes and Laughton Levels for the drainage of flood water, the river at times being subject to floods. These culverts appeared to have been made use of from time to time for the purposes of drainage. They were originally open but had at some time or other been arched over. A proper system of drainage was laid by the Corporation of Lewes after applying for a loan in 1900. These original culverts were open at both ends and communicated in four places with the river. The new recently installed system discharged into the river in one place and, because Cliffe was so low lying, the sewage was pumped by an electric-powered pump. The Council received no complaints of nuisances from the river. The severe epidemic of typhoid fever in 1873-1875 was found to be due to contaminated water from Lewes Waterworks Company, not due to any river water or sewage. The Water Company consequently altered their source of supply'...[38].

Maintenance in the 19th century to the 20th century

The modern world and a rising population were having effects on The Levels. In 1833 the first Lewes Waterworks Company was funded by a hundred contributors, and a pumping station was built on a one-acre parcel of brookland in the former meadows of 'The Cannells' near Southover. The water was pumped up to a reservoir at St Anne's to feed down to properties in Lewes. By 1845 the Brighton to Lewes railway was constructed just north of the waterworks and the Priory site.

The Newhaven Harbour and Lower Ouse Navigation Act 1847 meant that in the future there would be a separate board of Trustees, who levied their water scot for the harbour, sea walls and river entrance. The Watercourt for the other districts feared that the flood defences on the coast might prove inadequate or poorly maintained, so annual inspections were carried out between Newhaven and The Buckle. The financial arrangements for the commission was at this period placed in the hands of a treasurer, Major Harold Parminter Molineux, director of Barclays Bank, Lewes. All the monies for the water scots collected from landowners on The Levels were duly paid into the bank at set dates in the financial year.

The Great Sluice leading from Kingston Sewer (now called Celery Sewer) to Rodmell had 'blown-up' in June 1866 so that a breach was made in the river bank 'whereby the low lands' of the parishes of Southover, Kingston, Iford and Rodmell were flooded. A scot of 18s an acre was levied on the landowners for additional repair costs:-

Mr John Verrall, Southover, 101 acres

Rev. John Goring, Kingston, 134 acres

Earl de la Warr, Iford, 133 acres

Mrs Rosseter, Iford 54 acres

Mrs Rosseter, Iford, 62 acres

Henry Ridge, Iford, 83 acres

Earl Abergavenny, Rodmell, 166 acres.

By 1887 the Rodmell Sluice was reported to be in decay once again. After deliberation by the Commissioners, it was decided to add an auxiliary sluice to the south of the Great Sluice, with the cost to be borne by the landowners of The Levels from Kingston to Rodmell. A scot of 3s was levied to pay for the additional sluice. In 1888 it was reported to be working well, with The Levels having 'no special damage'. Further improvements had to be made to the mechanism of these sluices into the main river, evidently the balance between the levels of the fresh water fed into the brookland and the inflow of the tidal river was complex. In 1913 the Great Sluice door needed replacing and had to be fixed 3 inches lower for letting the water out. Also, the auxiliary sluice required a lock and key 'to prevent interference by unauthorised persons'.

During the time of the Great War, labour was short for the maintenance of The Levels and German prisoners of war were employed on cleansing and clearing. In 1919 a 'Crab' was fixed to aid the lifting of the heavy iron tide flap of the auxiliary sluice at the Rodmell outfall. Extensive casting and shoresetting was done at the east end of the great sewer, and was reported to be of great benefit though with heavy costs, but was considered to be worthwhile. In 1904 the Borough sewage works were developed on land close to the Cockshut to the east where the stream exits into the river Ouse. The members of the Watercourt viewed this latter development 'with apprehension' and sought legal and professional advice.

The Commissioners in 1920 were considering using concrete pipes instead of 'wooden trunks'. In 1921 the annual report states 'the general condition of The Levels from an agricultural point of view shows a very great deterioration when compared with the condition twenty years ago, due entirely to the failure of occupiers to carry out proper drainage works. The 'high farming' period flourished through the 19th century until economic change and depression from 1870 onwards altered the use of farmland. More housing was being built along roads adjacent to the brooklands, and sewage and run-offs were potential hazards to the water quality. Dairy herds and summer grazing adapted to the abundant grass growth, but brought maintenance problems. Foul water up to Glynde Reach, due to Lewes sewage brought up by the tides to Edlee, was affecting the drinking water of the 'milch cows' in Firle brooks as reported in 1918. Traces of sewage were noticed coming into the ditches in 1924 from the village of Kingston and Kingstonville, the latter, a post-war development on Kingston Ridge. A letter on the matter was sent to the Clerk of Newhaven District Council. Seventeen occupiers were given notice of the bad condition of their ditches and outlets. Rushes were appearing in many fresh places and 'the keeping of large herds of milch cows in the Levels militates against keeping the surface drains in good condition'. The banks of soft silty clays were easily broken by the hooves and the weight of the cows as they climbed down to drink water, and consequently crumbled and obstructed the ditches. Stock should be kept off the marshland from December to April. It was reckoned that unobstructed ditches greatly enhanced the cubic capacity of holding floodwater, keeping the grassland polders drained. It was reckoned that ditches adding up to 60 miles in length over 800 acres (425 ha) 'if properly cast would hold many thousands of tons of water'. The Annual Report of 1925 records serious flooding, with an annual rainfall of 48 inches, far more than the average of 33 inches. By 1928 the Committee recognised the serious depression in agriculture and determined to keep the water scot as low as possible. The year 1932 was described as 'in these difficult times'.

In August 1936 contractors for Lewes Borough Council commenced work on the Stanley Turner recreation ground near Southover, on the former meadows of 'The Cannells'. The erection of the pavilion was of concern in case it might discharge sewage into the Cockshut stream, which fed the brookland and the waterworks nearby. While these works were taking place, the year 1935-1936 was recorded as 'the wettest in memory', consequently the banks at the upper end were slipping into the stream because of raising of the ground and making earth banks.

The centuries of efforts from labouring men digging and shovelling, heaving and humping was to change. An appointed group from the River Board went to Pevensey Levels in 1938 to view a mechanical excavator and was 'very impressed'. A Priestman Drag-Line Cub was duly purchased and its first job was on the Pells Cut on 5 March 1938. Thereafter, the excavator was hired out to farmers in The Levels for ditch clearing. Subsequent reports record the locations of the excavator working at various sites in the Ouse valley. On the 10 November 1939 it was reported that the excavator had stopped work since the 3 September, as all three men had been called up for war service. Only two elderly men were regularly working on The Levels, and the excavator was stored on a dry bank at Edlee up Glynde Reach. However, a new crew was found and trained, and in 1942 the excavator was repairing bomb damage to the river bank at Asham. The excavator continued to do effective clearance and its location was the principal entry in the final stages of the records of Internal Drainage Board. In 1950, the last year, is written 'all the sewers for which the Board is responsible have been cleared out by the Excavator within the last three years, including all the main sewers in Laughton Levels the upper part of the Cockshut stream and the top of Kingston sewer'[39].

POSTSCRIPT

Since the autumn of 2000 when again all of Cliffe was flooded, including the commercial area on the former Malling Brooks to the north, which caused much harm, damage and financial loss, there have been ongoing discussions between various agencies – the Environment Agency, East Sussex County Council, the District Councils and the local Land Drainage Committee. Consultations have taken place in Lewes Town Hall with the inhabitants of Cliffe and Lewes. The Flood Defence Strategy (March 2002) was drawn up with the following proposals:

- raising the flood defence walls through the town

- downstream flood storage south of Lewes on the brookland as far as White Wall at Southease

- upstream storage north of Lewes with embankment on the flood plain. As Malling Brooks is now occupied with housing and commerce, this would mean brookland below Landport, Offham and Hamsey.

Decisions on how to proceed with solution of the prevention of flood episodes caused by exceptional rainfall, high spring tides and rising sea levels, continue to test the expertise of the Environment Agency. The function of the flood plain, including The Levels with its drainage ditches, sewers and sluices, is an essential part of the successful management of the river system. These past records give an indication of the complexity of the problem that has taxed people's thinking for over six hundred years [40].

REFERENCES

1. J. Craddock, (1976), The Anglo-Saxon Cemetry *SAC 117, 85-102*. M. Lyne, (1977), *Lewes Priory, Excavations by R. Lewis* 1969-82, Lewes Priory Trust, 15, mentions 'abraided Roman and Saxon shards in clayey soil beneath the southern apse floor'.

2. The majority of the vills/settlements are recorded in J. Morris, (ed) (1976), *Domesday Book*, (Chichester), except for Kingston which was included in the Iford entry 12,3 and Piddinghoe and Meeching, which were not listed, but they are recorded in *The Chartulary of the Priory of St Pancras*, SRS 38, 161, c.1150. Denton was part of Bishopstone, held by the Bishop of Chichester, and Southerham was similarly an ecclesiastical holding of the Archbishop of Canterbury.

3. *An Historical Atlas of Sussex* ed. K. Leslie and B. Short, (1999), presents clearly in chapters 8-11 early sites and settlements, with references. Excavation of a Neolithic Causewayed Enclosure on Offham Hill by P. Drewett, *Procedings of Prehistoric Society* 43 (1977) 201-41. Itford Bronze Age settlement report is in *SAC* 101 by G. Burstow and G. Holleyman and the report of The Bronze Age Cemetry and Barrow, Itford Hill by E. Holden, (1972), *SAC* 115 (1977) 1-241. The excavations at Newhaven by M. Bell are in *SAC* 114 (1976), 18-305. Based on earlier investigations The Caburn Project has resulted in further analysis by P. Drewett and S. Hamilton in *SAC* 137 (1999) 7. The final report for the Preston Court villa has not been published in the *SAC*, but there is a report by D. Rudling in *Britannia* 1987-1993. Barcombe Villa excavation is ongoing, and reports so far are in *Past and Present* No.95 Dec 2001, No.98 Dec 2002, No.105 Apr 2005.

4. C.A. Holleyman (1956) An Early British Agricultural Village Site on Highdole Hill near Telscombe *SAC* 77, 202-221 and L. Field and C.F. Hawkes (1939) on Castle Hill, Newhaven *SAC* 80, 292. O. Bedwin, (1976) *SAC* 116, 241-256 Excavation of a Roman site at Ranscombe Hill.

5.   Report by G. Thomas on finds and excavations on the edge of South Malling on Stoneham farmland in *Past and Present* (April 2002) also N. Norris (1956) *SAC* 94, 10-12. The Archaeology South-East report *Lewes-Newhaven Pipeline, ref 879* (2000). The burials at Loover Hill, by Glynde Bridge were found by the Rev. de Saint Croix and written in *SAC* 26 (1868) 51-54. For Anglo-Saxon burhs – D. Hill and A. Rumble (1996). *The Defence of Wessex: The Burghal Hidage and Anglo Saxon Fortification* (Manchester) 84. For a short notice on these Southease burials see *SAC* 5, 204. For reports by G. Thomas of the discoveries at Bishopstone *Sussex Past and Present* no 105 April 2005, No 109 August 2006.

6.   ESCC Archaeology Department has these drawn field plans. R. Coates, (1990) *Some Place Names on the Downland Fringe*, Brighton: Younsmere Press. R. Coates, (1991). Roman Villa Site at Beddingham – Local Place Names *LAG Newsletter 97*.

7.   M. Gelling (1997) *Signposts to the Past*, (Chichester), 125. D. Saunders, (1998), The Saxon *TUN* in *Locus Focus* 2, No. 1, Sussex Place Names Net, University of Sussex. J. Morris (1976) 2,1. 7,1. 10,3. Southease charter, AD 966, transcription in the church.

8.   ed. L.F. Salzman (1958), *The Customary of the Archbishop of Canterbury's Manors in Sussex*, SRS 72. Remembering 'Round-the-Down': topographical perspectives on early settlement and land use at Southerham near Lewes, G. Vines and F. Price *SAC* 143, (2005), 117-134.

9.   S. Kelly ed (1998), *Anglo Saxon Charters vi Charters of Selsey*.

10.   This idea is discussed by T. Williamson, (2003) in *Shaping Medieval Landscapes* (Windgather) 40-43. I believe that P. F. Brandon has also considered these linear boundaries to be early.

11.   E. Holden and T. Hudson (1981), Saltmaking in the Adur Valley *SAC* 119, 117-148, – describes processes and physical remains. Salthouses are recorded in J. Morris ed (1976) *Domesday*

Book: Sussex, 124. A. H. Smith (1970), English Place Name Elements, *English Place Name Society*, 251, 1, Cambridge University Press.

12.   These acres of meadows are in the Domesday record, 1086, see J. Morris. South Heighton's meadow rights were of course included in the 130 acres at Southease.

13.   SRS 38, 163, 169, 21, etc.

14.   P.F. Brandon, (1971). Agriculture and the effects of flood and weather during the late Middle Ages, *SAC* 100, 69-93. B. Moffat, (1986), The environment of Battle Abbey estates (East Sussex) in medieval times; a re-evaluation using analysis of pollen and sediments, *Landscape History* 8, 77-89. For the site at Stutfall, B. Cunliffe, (1980), Excavations at the Roman fort at Lympne, Kent 1986-78. *Britannia* 11, 227-288.

15.   SRS 38, 21 and 50. M. Lyne, (1997), *Lewes Priory Excavations by Richard Lewis* 1969-1982, 1 and 2. F. Anderson, *le Système hydraulique et lavabo du prieuré de Lewes* 1992) Sussex Archaeological Society Library 942.25 (LEW).

16.   SRS *38, 162.*

17.   Early Curia Regis Rolls 1199-1230 *Seldon Society*, 21,287,328,329 to be found KD 530 SEL, University of Sussex Library.

18.   A. Dulley, (1966), The Level and Port of Pevensey in the Middle Ages *SAC* 104, 26-45. Rev. E. Turner, (1867), Statutes of the Marshes of Pevensey and Romney *SAC* 18, 42-53. Also L.F. Salzman, (1910), The Inning of Pevensey Levels *SAC* 53, 32-60.

19.   Sir H. Ellis, (1858), Commissions of Sewers for Lewes Levels *SAC* 10, 95-97 and VCH 2, 69. *The Book of Bartholomew Bolney* ed M. Clough SRS 63, (1964), 56, 86. *The Chartulary of the High Church of Chichester* ed W.D. Peckham SRS 46 (1942) 199. P. F. Brandon (1971), The Origin of Newhaven and the Drainage of Lewes and Laughton Levels, *SAC* 109, 93-106. Lists of names, ESRO Glynde MS 84.

20. The topic of the river origins was presented at a Symposium at the University of Sussex, 11 March 2006 by Rendell Williams. Also read *The Weald* by S. W. Wooldridge and F. Goldring, (5th imp. 1972) Collins, London. D. K. C. Jones, *The Geomorphology of the British Isles The South East and Southern England*, London (1981) 40,41.

21. J. Morris ed (1976), *Domesday Book: Sussex*, Phillimore 1-2,1*a*, 2 1*f*. 11-121. G. R. J. Jones, Multiple Estates and Early Settlement, ed P H Sawyer, *Medieval Settlement* Edward Arnold (1976), 26-34. D. Hill and A. Rumble (1996), *The Defence of Wessex: The Burghal Hidage and Anglo Saxon Fortification*, Manchester, 84.

22. *The Customary of the Archbishop of Canterbury's Manors in Sussex* ed L. F. Salzman, SRS 72 (1958) 115, 116. Sidney Stokes, Notes and Queries, *SAC* 73 (1952). D. Rudling, Excavations at Cliffe, 1987 and 1988. *SAC* **129** (1991), 179. ESRO, M. Gardiner, *Medieval Settlement and Society in the Eastern Sussex Weald before 1420*, unpub. Ph.D. thesis, University of London (1995).

23. Minute Books of the Commission of Sewers and Laughton Levels in the Archive of the Sussex River Authority

     ESRO   *SRA*6/2/1 June 1626 – August 1703 + Index

     *SRA*6/2/2 July 1704 – June 1764 + Index

     *SRA*6/2/3 June 1765 – July 1824

     *SRA*6/2/4 Index to 2/3 above

     *SRA*6/2/5 June 1825 – October 1844

     *SRA*6/2/6 Index to 2/5 above

     *SRA*6/2/7 June 1845 – April 1876

     *SRA*6/2/8 Index to 2/7 above

     *SRA*6/2/9 June 1876 – February 1895

     *SRA*6/2/10 Index to 2/9 above

     *SRA*6/2/11 June 1895 – Feb 1913

SRA6/2/12 June 1913 – Feb 1930

SRA6/2/13 June 1930 – Sept 1950

24.   ESRO John de Ward, 1620, *Map of the Levels* A 2187.

ESRO A. Everenden, 1633, *Northease Court Farm* Aber 62 acc 363/62. The new Act for improving Newhaven harbour is quoted in *SAC* 64 (1923) Notes and Queries 195.

25.   VCH 7, 9. Rev. Edward Turner, The Marchant Diary, *SAC* **25,** (1873), 194. ESRO *SRA6/9/5* (1752) Cliffe sewers and labour.

26.   John Smeaton's drawn plan of proposed improvements 1766, is enclosed.

27.   ESRO *SRA6/14/8* correspondence between Rt. Hon. T. Pelham and Mr Jessop. ESRO *SRA6/9/8*, River Book, work paid for, June 1774 – November 1779. ESRO *SRA6/13/6* Map by Wm. Figg 1832, shows further river straightening at the Ranscombe cut and past Itford brooks. The former meanders are marked on the present O.S. map.

28.   This part has been extracted from the commissioners' records and J. Farrant, The Lower Ouse Navigation 2, *Sussex Industrial Archaeology Society,* Newsletter No. 4, October 1974. C. Brent, (1995), *Georgian Lewes*, and Alan F. Hill (1991), *The Lower Ouse Navigation*, 1834-1967.

29.   ESRO *SWA12/1/1* A Survey and A Measurement of Lewes and Laughton Levels made by order of Commissioners of Sewers in 1791 by Thos. Budgen, revised and corrected by Wm. Figg 1827. ESRO A5179/28, The Second District by T. Budgen, 1791. Also this data is used by J. H. Farrant in *SAC* **110** (1972) 44-60.

30.   M. Overton, (2001), *Agricultural Revolution in England*, Cambridge University Press, 191-2. P. F. Brandon and B. Short, (1990). *The South East from* AD1000, London 202-261. B. Short, The South East, 270-313 in *The Agrarian History of England and Wales* 5(1) 1640-1750 ed J. Thirsk (1984) Cambridge University Press.

31. Plan of Lord Sheffield's Farm Yard is in Rev. A. Young, Appendix 480. I. Nairn and N. Pevsner, (1973), *The Buildings of England: Sussex*, 605, 606, 301.

32. For more detail on Petworth and Lord Egremont see Rev. A. Young (1813) (rep 1970) *General View of the Agriculture of the County of Sussex*, chapters 7 & 8, Ellman 108-112, Carr 93, 94. S. Farrant (1978), John Ellman of Glynde. *Agricultural History Review* Part 2. For more on productivity see *Land, Labour and Livestock* ed B. M. S. Campbell & M. Overton (1991), Manchester University Press.

33. Rev. Young (1813), 157-161. For Ellman and The Shine, ESRO ROB 1/1/33(i).

34. E. Kerridge (1953), The sheepfold in Wiltshire and the floating of water meadows, *Economic History Review* 6 282-9. Rev. Young (1813), 'watered meadows' 222. WSRO T. Marchant, Plan and Survey of Kingston 1773, Wiston No. 5649, 5650, and Working Notebook 1760, Wiston no. 5651. ESRO Plan of 'The Cannells' by Wm. Figg, c.1850. See also the *Book of John Rowe*, SRS 34, ed W. Godfrey (1928), for rights on brookland at Rodmell, 57, 62 and at Northease with Iford, 69, 70. References to cutting of meadows are in *The Book of Bartholomew Bolney*, ed. M. Clough SRS 63 (1964), 32, 56, 86, dated c1458. Also *SAC* 3, (1850), Wm. Figg, Manorial Customs of Southease with Heighton, and SRS 34, 222, 223. *SAC* 4 (1851), Wm. Figg, The Tenantry Customs in Sussex – The Drinker Acre. See also photograph 1928 in Geological Survey Memoir, Lewes, of the partitions of meadow still existing of 'The Cannells', Kingston.

35. ESRO Thomas Budgen 1790, Draft book references of survey of Lewes and Laughton Levels, by parish and occupiers *AMS 6164/3* and plans *AMS 6164/4*. ESRO *SWA 12/1/1*, A Survey and a Measurement of Lewes and Laughton Levels made by order of Commissioners of Sewers in 1791 by Thomas Budgen revised and corrected by Wm. Figg 1827.

36. ESRO Kingston and Iford 1830, 2,527 acres, Enclosure Award QDD/G/E4. ESRO Telscombe 1810, 690 acres. ESRO

Southease 1836, 758 acres. Articles of Agreement between proprietors of Iford Manor 1670, ESRO ROB 1/1/7.

37.   M. Overton, (2001), chapter 5. B. Short, Landownership in Victorian Sussex 98, 99 in *'An Historical Atlas of Sussex'* ed K. Leslie and B. Short (1999). P. F. Brandon and B. Short, (1990), *The South East from* AD*1000*, 317. S. Farrant, (1977). *The Role of Landowners and Tenants* and *Changing Agricultural Practice in the Valley of the River Ouse, 1780-1930*, unpub. Ph.D. thesis University of London (SAS library and ESRO)

38.   ESRO C10/1/1 Cliffe Improvement Act, 9 Geo.IV 1828. ESRO NRA 12/2 Corporation of Lewes. *Brief by Counsel against Rivers Pollution Prevention Act 1876*. Plan of the sewers of Cliffe, ESRO ACC 3412/5/1

39.   All this section is drawn from the later records 1845-1950 of the Commission of Sewers, see reference 23.

40.   Environment Agency. *Environment Report: River Ouse Catchment Flood Management Plan 2006*, Guildbourne House, Worthing.

FURTHER READING

Brandon, P.F. (1971) Agriculture and the Effects of Floods and Weather at Barnehorne, Sussex during the late Middle Ages, *SAC* **109**, 69-93.

Brandon, P.F. (1971) The Origin of Newhaven and the Drainage of Lewes and Laughton Levels. *SAC* **109**, 94-106.

Brandon P.F. (1998) *The South Downs*, Chichester.

Brandon, P.F and Short, B. (1990) *The South East from* AD*1000*, London.

Brent, C. (1993) *Georgian Lewes 1714-1830*, Lewes.

Brent C. (2004) *Pre-Georgian Lewes 890-1714*, Lewes.

Clough, M. ed. (1964) *The Book of Bartholomew Bolney*, SRS **63**.

Drewett, P., Rudling, D., Gardiner, M. (1988) *The South East to* AD*1000*, London.

Dulley, A. (1996). The Level and Port of Pevensey in the Middle Ages SAC **104**, 26-45.

Ellis, Sir H. (1858) Commissioners of Sewers for the Lewes Levels *SAC* **10**, 95-99.

Farrant, J.H. (1972) The Evolution of Newhaven Harbour and the Lower Ouse before 1800 *SAC* **110**, 44-60.

Farrant, S. (1977) *The Role of Landowners and Tenants and Changing Agricultural Practice in the Valley of the River Ouse 1780-1930*, unpub. Ph.D. thesis, University of London.

Farrant S. (1978) John Ellman of Glynde, *Agricultural History Review, part 2.*

Gardiner, M. (1995) *Medieval Settlement and Society in the Eastern Weald before 1420*, unpub. Ph.D. thesis, University of London.

Gelling, M. and Cole, A. (2000) *The Landscape of Place Names*, Stamford.

Gibbs, D.F. and Farrant, J.H. (1970-1971) The Upper Ouse Navigation 1790-1868, *Sussex Industrial Society.*

Godfrey, W.H. ed. (1928) *The Book of John Rowe*, SRS **34.**

Hill, A. (1991) *The Lower Ouse Navigation 1832-1967*, private publication.

Hill, D. and Rumble, A. (1996) *The Defence of Wessex: The Burghal Hidage and Anglo-Saxon Fortification*, Manchester.

Jones, D. K. C. (1981) *The Geomorphology of the British Isles, The South East and Southern England*, London.

Kerridge, E. (1967) *The Agricultural Revolution*, London.

Lyne, M. (1999) *Lewes Priory: Excavations by Richard Lewis 1969-1982*, Lewes Priory Trust.

Leslie, K. and Short, B. ed. (1999) *An Historical Atlas of Sussex*, Chichester.

Mawer, A. and Stenton, F.M. ed. (1930) *The Place Names of Sussex, English Place Name Society 7*, Cambridge.

Morris, J. ed. (1996) *Domesday Book: Sussex*, Chichester.

Overton, M. (1996) *Agricultural Revolution in England: the Transformation of the Agrarian Economy 1500-1850*, Cambridge.

Peckham, W.D. ed. (1942) *The Chartulary of the High Church of Chichester*, SRS **46.**

Pevsner, N. and Nairn, I. (1973) *The Buildings of England: Sussex*, Harmonsworth.

Rudling, D. (1991) Excavations at Cliffe, *SAC* **129**, 165-182.

Salzman, L.F. ed. (1940) *Victoria County History, Sussex vol.7*, London.

Salzman, L.F. ed. (1932 and 1934) *The Chartulary of the Priory of St Pancras*, SRS **38** and SRS **40.**

Salzman, L.F. ed. (1958) *The Customary of the Archbishop of Canterbury's Manors in Sussex*, SRS **72.**

Short, B. (1984) The South East in ed. J. Thirsk *The Agrarian History of England and Wales 1640-1750*, Cambridge.

Thorley, A. (1971) Vegetational History in the Vale of the Brooks, in R. B. G. Williams ed. *A Guide to Sussex Excursions*, Institute of British Geographers Conference, (Jan 1971), 47 – 50.

Turner, Rev. E. (1867) Statutes of the Marshes of Pevensey and Romney, *SAC 18*, 42-53.

Young, Rev. A. (1813, reprint 1970) *General View of Agriculture of the County of Sussex*.

INDEX